# Three Simple Questions
## Leader Guide

# Three
# Simple Questions

———————m———————

## KNOWING THE GOD
## OF LOVE, HOPE,
## AND PURPOSE

## Rueben P. Job

## Leader Guide
## Pamela C. Hawkins

**Abingdon Press / Nashville**

THREE SIMPLE QUESTIONS:
LEADER GUIDE


Copyright © 2011 by Abingdon Press

Scripture quotations, unless otherwise indicated, are from the New Revised Standard Version of the Bible, copyrighted © 1989 by the Division of Christian Education of the National Council of the Churches of Christ in the United States of America, and are used by permission.


This book is printed on acid-free, elemental chlorine-free paper.

ISBN 978-1-4267-4263-7

11 12 13 14 15 16 17 18 19 20—10 9 8 7 6 5 4 3 2 1

MANUFACTURED IN THE UNITED STATES OF AMERICA

# Contents

# Preface

It is a privilege for me to write this Leader Guide to accompany Rueben P. Job's new book, *Three Simple Questions: Knowing the God of Love, Hope, and Purpose,* because Bishop Job has been a mentor and friend for many years.

I first met Rueben Job when he graciously agreed to be my field education supervisor as I began studies at Vanderbilt Divinity School in the early 1990s. My field education placement was with The Upper Room, a publishing program and ministry of The United Methodist Church, where Rueben was working in one of his many post-retirement ministries of Christian spiritual formation. At the time, I had absolutely no idea who he was, only that he and I shared interests in prayer and the spiritual life, and that he was willing to help me learn about both.

For a year, as I worked to juggle school and family and employment and faith, Rueben faithfully had my name on his calendar so that we could sit and talk, pray and work—student and guide. Several years later, when at last I had completed all official requirements to become an ordained elder in the church, Rueben Job participated in my ordination. Ever since then, through all the appointments, moves, ministries, joys, and struggles that have come and gone for us both, Rueben has continued to be a guide for me. There has never been a question about faith or life or call or hope that I could not ask Rueben. He has always urged me to trust the mystery and power of questions.

So to be asked to write a Leader Guide for a work that is near to Rueben's heart has been a remarkable and humbling request. And to be asked to do this for a book entitled *Three Simple Questions,* honoring and illumining the spiritual practice of asking and living into questions, a practice in which he has been my guide throughout our friendship, is pure grace.

As many of you know, *Three Simple Questions* follows Rueben's previous and widely acclaimed work, *Three Simple Rules: A Wesleyan Way of Living* (Abingdon, 2007). In *Three Simple Rules,* Rueben took time to remind us that the simplicity of three Wesleyan rules—Do No Harm; Do Good; Stay in Love with God—carries the "power to change the world."[1]

With *Three Simple Questions,* Rueben now challenges our faith, not with three simple, world-changing rules; but with three simple, world-changing questions:

Who is God?
Who am I?
Who are we together?

These questions are important to us if we want to find a better way to follow Jesus in greater faithfulness and fidelity to the God of love, hope, and purpose.

Rueben Job believes with all his heart that most of us want to find this better way. So do I. *Three Simple Questions* is a gift and guide for us to do so.

Pamela C. Hawkins

# Using *Three Simple Questions* as a Small-Group Resource

*Three Simple Questions* can be used as a resource for individual reading and reflection, as well as for a six-session small-group study. When used with a small group, this Leader Guide offers content options for a 60-minute or 90-minute format. For small-group use, participants will be asked to read part of the *Three Simple Questions* book before each session. A variety of activities and practices are provided for group leaders to read and select prior to a group session.

Material in this Leader Guide is recommended for groups of ten or twelve, but can also be adapted for use with a larger Sunday school class or gathering. At the end of the guide you'll also find outlines for using *Three Simple Questions* as retreat content for either a one-day or three-day retreat (see pages 60-62).

This leader guide is designed to help group leaders arrange and combine activities according to the group experience and participation. Optional and alternative activities are provided for each session, so that a leader can supplement or substitute as desired.

Preparation by participants for each session will involve about thirty minutes of reading, and group leaders will need up to an hour of preparation in order to read, view, and select material. Again, group sessions are designed for either a 60-minute or 90-minute format, but this, too, is adaptable

The group leader will read the same material in *Three Simple Questions* as participants, but will also read and prepare with content from this Leader Guide.

## Session Formats

This Leader Guide presents a plan for six small-group sessions to be used with Rueben P. Job's book, *Three Simple Questions*.

Each session plan includes activities for a 60-minute format and a 90-minute format. Leaders and groups can choose to follow one of these two formats, or they can treat the activities as a menu from which to select and create their own format, according to the group's time constraints and learning styles.

### 60-Minute Format

| | |
|---|---|
| Opening: Welcome and Prayer | 5 minutes |
| Video and Discussion | 15 minutes |
| Book Discussion | 15 minutes |
| Spiritual Practice | 15 minutes |
| Closing: Reflection and Prayer | 5-10 minutes |

### 90-Minute Format

| | |
|---|---|
| Opening: Welcome and Prayer | 5 minutes |
| Video and Discussion | 15 minutes |
| Book Discussion | 15 minutes |
| Spiritual Practice | 15 minutes |
| Prayer Practice | 15 minutes |
| Creative Practice | 20-30 minutes |
| Closing: Reflection and Prayer | 5-10 minutes |

# Activities

To help leaders and groups choose the format that works best for them, here are descriptions of each activity:

**Before the Group Meets**
A summary of what the leader needs to do in preparation for the upcoming session.

**Opening: Welcome and Prayer** (5 minutes)
Includes an introductory summary of the session and an opening liturgy of Scripture, silence, and prayer. It is recommended that for the first two sessions, the leader is responsible for this section, but may want to invite participants to assist after Session 2.

**Video and Discussion** (15 minutes)
The group views together the session video, which is 6-8 minutes long. The group then reflects together on the ideas presented in the video.

**Book Discussion** (15 minutes each)
Two options:

*Group Reflection*
This element invites participants to engage more deeply with the material read for the session. For some sessions, the leader is asked to guide the whole group in reflection; for other sessions, participants may first be asked to get into pairs or triads to reflect.

*Silent Reflection and Group Discussion*
This element invites participants to spend additional time reviewing and discussing reading material for each session.

**Spiritual Practice** (15 minutes)
This activity offers participants the opportunity to experience a unique spiritual practice that is selected for ways in which it illumines the reading content and question. These are not intended to provide extensive practice, but to introduce participants to spiritual practices they may wish to use on their own at a later time.

**Prayer Practice** (15 minutes)
Participants will be given a handout about a prayer practice. The group leader will guide participants through the practice and a discussion about the practice. Each prayer practice has been selected because of a way in which it can help participants live into the "three simple questions."

**Creative Practice** (20-30 minutes)
This element invites participants to engage with the reading material and three simple questions in some ways that may draw upon less verbal and linear processes. Some visual, spatial, and kinesthetic consideration has been given to this element. Often for these options, the group leader will need to bring some additional materials that are noted in the section "Before the Group Meets."

**Closing: Reflection and Prayer** (5-10 minutes)
Each session closes with a single-word spiritual practice of reflection, followed by a time of prayer, blessing, and peace.

# Session 1
# Introduction

## Before the Group Meets

Prayerfully read the Preface of *Three Simple Questions* and the material in this leader guide for Session 1. Preview the video segment for Session 1.

If possible, and especially for Session 1, call or e-mail each participant to welcome them and to confirm details about location, time, reading assignment (Preface), and materials to bring to the session.

**For Session 1 the participant will need:**
- A copy of *Three Simple Questions*
- Pen or pencil
- Journal, notebook, or writing paper

**For Session 1 the leader will need:**
- A plan for how the room should be set up for the session
- A few extra copies of *Three Simple Questions*
- Candle for prayer times, and a lighter or matches
- DVD player and monitor
- At least one Bible (recommend Common English Bible)

- Pencils and pens
- Extra paper for notes
- (Optional) If your group will be doing the Prayer Practice, prepare handout copies of "Prayer of Silent Listening."
- (Optional) If your group will be doing the Creative Practice, bring a blank sheet of paper for each person.
- (Optional) Light refreshments if the group leader desires to provide them

*Note that activities not included in the basic 60-minute format are marked below with an asterisk (\*). However, leaders are free to use any of the activities best suited to their group's time constraints and learning styles.*

# Opening: Welcome and Prayer (5 minutes)

**Leader:** (*read aloud or summarize*)

This is a six-week study and conversation group based upon Rueben P. Job's book, *Three Simple Questions*. For each session we will read one part of the book before we gather, and then we will discuss, reflect upon, and experience the reading. The central elements of this study are the three simple yet profound questions that Rueben Job believes can lead us to a new understanding of God, ourselves, and the whole human family. The questions are:

Who is God?
Who am I?
Who are we together?

As we explore these questions together, we will not only discuss them, but we will also learn and experience spiritual practices that allow these questions to lead us into a more faithful way of living as part of the body of Christ in the world. In other words, these questions can lead us to become more faithful followers of Jesus.

Before we open with prayer, let's introduce ourselves to each other. (*Invite participants to introduce themselves at this time.*)

We will open each week with a time of welcome and prayer, so I invite us to enter into silence as we light a candle representing the light of Christ, always present.

## Liturgy

*Opening Prayer:*
We welcome you, O God, into this time we spend together, that as our questions are spoken and answers come to light and life, we may listen for you through and with each other. By your grace, and with the power of the Holy Spirit, help us follow and trust the better way of Jesus. Amen.

*Reading from Psalms:* Read aloud Psalm 62:1.

*Silence*

*Scripture Reading:* Read aloud 1 John 4:7-9.

*Silence*

*Prayer for Guidance:*
God of hope, we thank you for drawing each of us from our separate lives into this small community of faith. You know our stories—the curves, contours, and rough places from which we come—and still you create through us a new story formed and imprinted by your ever-fervent love. You know our questions—those we risk out loud and those we cling to in our innermost selves—and still you urge us to freely wonder together with head and heart. Help us remember, find, and follow a better way than our ways, O God. Help us rediscover the better way of Jesus. Amen

# Video and Discussion (15 minutes)

Introduce the Session 1 video by describing the format. The video is six to eight minutes long and is made up of three parts:
- Voices asking questions
- Story by Rueben Job
- Hosted presentation

After watching the video, lead the group in a discussion:

- What or who stood out to you as you heard the voices?
- What images or circumstances in the world today did Rueben Job's story bring to mind for you?
- How do you respond to the idea that "three simple questions" can lead us to a closer relationship with God and our whole human family?

## Book Discussion (15 minutes)

Choose one of the following:

### Group Reflection

Ask participants to turn to pages 9-10 of the Preface to *Three Simple Questions,* where the following quotations can be found. Using the book or the paragraph below, read the quotations aloud twice, while the group members listen, and then begin a time of reflection in the whole group with the questions that follow.

We cannot escape the divisions, anger, hatred, and violence that are tearing apart the world that God so loved. Neither can we avoid the truth that so much of the anger, hatred, distrust, and division prevalent in the world has invaded the church. In our honest moments, we know that this is not the way we want to live, should live, or are called to live by the God we have come to know through Jesus Christ. . . . But what are we to do?

- What words or images come to mind for you, as these quotations are read?
- What do these quotations tell us about God?
- What do they tell us about human beings?

### Silent Reflection and Group Discussion

Ask participants to review silently the Preface of *Three Simple Questions* (pages 9-10). Are there words, images, or phrases that stopped, puzzled, inspired, or troubled them? Allow two or three minutes for this silent review. Then invite each group member to share one question, insight, or reflection with the group.

Before sharing begins, encourage others to listen to the person who is sharing and to resist responding. Then, after each person who wishes to do so has shared, invite the group to discuss what they have heard, using an opening question such as "What did we hear?"

## Spiritual Practice (15 minutes)

*Before moving into the spiritual practice, invite participants to stand and stretch for a moment as a way of transition and refreshment.*

This section is designed to help participants become familiar with a variety of spiritual practices—in particular, practices that illumine each week's reading. For example, as we begin our time together, the spiritual practice of hospitality can serve as a beautiful introduction to the three simple questions we will share. Each participant will need a journal, notebook, or piece of writing paper and a pen or pencil. As leader, you will want to manage the time carefully during this practice.

**Leader:** (*read aloud or summarize*)

The practice of Christian hospitality, though often relegated in our minds to providing a greeting at the door or refreshments after worship, is far more expansive and deep. At its core, hospitality is about offering an open welcome to all, especially all who are "other" than the welcoming ones. And so, for this first week of the group study, the practice of Christian hospitality is essential in order for the group to gather, form, and be formed by both the Spirit of God and by each other.

Listen to this quotation from author and Christian ethicist Christine Pohl:

> Hospitality is not so much a task as it is a way of living our lives and sharing ourselves. Although it involves responsibility and faithful performance of duties, hospitality emerges from a grateful heart; it is first a response of love and gratitude for God's love and welcome to us. Hospitality will not occur in any significant way in our

lives, homes, or churches unless we give it deliberate attention. . . .[2]

*Slowly read the following instructions to participants, giving time for each to be followed. As leader, you will need to pay attention to the time limit.*

### A Spiritual Practice of Hospitality

- In the next five minutes, invite group members to be in a time of silent, deliberate attention to the practice of hospitality. Tell them that this is the first step we must take to recover and enter into this often forgotten and misunderstood spiritual practice. Ask them during this time to reflect on experiences in which they either received or offered hospitality.
- After five minutes, ask group members to recall a time when they were the stranger, the "other," and someone extended loving hospitality to them. Allow one or two minutes for them to write about or sketch the situation.
- Next, ask the group to recall a time when they extended loving hospitality to a stranger. Who was the stranger, what was the setting, what was needed and offered? Again, allow one or two minutes to describe or sketch.
- After this time of remembering, spend the next few minutes as a group sharing some of the experiences that came to mind. As you do, make a list of qualities or characteristics of loving hospitality. Close the activity by reading back the list to the group.

## *Prayer Practice (15 minutes)

The following handout may be photocopied for group use:

## Prayer of Silent Listening

If we are truly open to becoming more serious about our understanding of God, self, and relationships, then we must make room for God. We must set aside distractions, premature answers, and rote practices. Just as hospitality begins with creating space for God and others, so too does prayer best begin by making room for God. So our first prayer practice is learning to listen for God's voice in silence.

In the book *Becoming a Praying Congregation: Churchwide Leadership Tools,* Rueben Job describes this prayer practice:

> With a note pad near, spend time in quiet listening for the voice of the One "who has nothing to learn from you but everything to tell you." Do not be distracted by the many images, ideas, and feelings that flood your silence. Simply call yourself back to attentiveness to God with a brief prayer or invitation, such as "Come, Holy Spirit," or offering, "Here I am, Lord," and continue the silent listening.[3]

Where better to begin our prayer together than by learning to listen in the silence for the voice of God? Perhaps, in silence, we can allow our three simple questions to become rooted in our hearts and heads in fresh and uncluttered ways.

Read once through the following guide, and then enter into silence and follow the steps listed.

- Get writing paper and a pencil or pen, and then find a comfortable position in which you can stay for at least ten minutes of silence.
- Call yourself to attend to God. It may help to use a simple prayer or invitation, such as "Come, Holy Spirit," or "Here I am, Lord." In silence, repeat this or other words of prayer over and over to help you bring God into your heart and mind.
- Gently set aside distractions that appear—"images, ideas, and feelings that naturally flood your silence." When these appear, do what you can to put them aside.
- Feel free to write down what you hear or experience as you pray. Resist analyzing or editing what you hear.
- After ten minutes, say "Amen." As you become more comfortable with this practice, extend the period of time.

When practicing with a group, engage in a conversation about how you experienced this prayer practice. What was it like for you? Spend a few minutes discussing your experience.

## *Creative Practice (20-30 minutes)

Each person will need a blank sheet of paper and a pencil or pen. Instruct participants to turn the paper with the long side at the top and bottom (landscape orientation) and to divide the paper into three equal columns. At the top of the first column write "Who is God?"; at the top of the middle column write "Who am I?"; and at the top of the third column write "Who are we together?"

Over the next ten minutes, invite participants to work in silence as they list qualities or attributes that come to mind from their personal experience of God, self, and their community. Encourage group members to resist editing what comes to mind and instead to be guided by the spirit of honesty. This is their list and no one else's. Single words and short phrases are best for this practice.

After ten minutes, instruct participants to gather into groups of three and, as they are willing, to share either how they experienced this activity or some of the qualities that came to mind, especially any surprising ones. Each person should have about five minutes to share.

Use the last few minutes for the whole group to report back about their discussions.

## Closing: Reflection and Prayer (5-10 minutes)

Invite participants into a closing time by asking each of them to choose one word that describes how they are feeling about the "Three Simple Questions" you will be exploring in the next few weeks. Assure participants that there is no right or wrong word, no need to be similar or different, but simply to share a word that comes to mind and heart as they explore these questions together. As leader, it will be helpful for you to share your word first, and then go around the group.

*Closing Prayers:* Ask if there are any prayers to be shared in the group and receive these.
*Lord's Prayer:* Pray together.

*Blessing:* May the God of love who made you, whisper to your soul that you are beloved and called to love one another and all of creation. May you have eyes to see and ears to hear that this is so. Go in peace.

As participants prepare to depart, remind them to read "Who Is God?" from *Three Simple Questions* in preparation for the next group session.

# Session 2
# Who Is God?

## Before the Group Meets

Prayerfully read "Who Is God?" in *Three Simple Questions,* as well as the material in this leader guide for Session 2. Preview the video segment for Session 2.

**For Session 2 the participant will need:**
- Copy of *Three Simple Questions*
- Pen or pencil
- Journal, notebook, or writing paper

**For Session 2 the leader will need:**
- A plan for how the room should be set up for the session
- A few extra copies of *Three Simple Questions*
- Candle for prayer times, and a lighter or matches
- DVD player and monitor
- At least one Bible (recommend Common English Bible)
- Pencils and pens
- Extra paper for notes

- (Optional) If your group will be doing the Prayer Practice, pre-pare handout copies of "Prayer of Imagination."
- (Optional) If your group will be doing the Creative Practice, bring a large index card for each person.
- (Optional) Light refreshments if the group leader desires to provide any

*Note that activities not included in the basic 60-minute format are marked below with an asterisk (\*). However, leaders are free to use any of the activities best suited to their group's time constraints and learning styles.*

## Opening Welcome and Prayer (5 minutes)

**Leader:** (*read aloud or summarize*)

Session 2 of this study is designed to foster conversation around the simple yet profound question "Who is God?" Each of us carries within us names and images for God, arising from our life experiences, stories, and beliefs. What is similar and what is different about God for each of us? In Jesus, how is our image of God shaped, revealed, and made known? Where does love fit into our image of God individually, communally, and globally? How does our answer to this question speak to what we believe about love or mercy or peace? This is what we will explore together during this session.

Now let us enter a time of silence as we light the candle that represents the light of Christ in the world and prepare for open-ing prayer.

### Liturgy

*Opening Prayer:*

We welcome you, O God, into this time we spend together, that as our questions are spoken and answers come to light and life, we may listen for you through and with each other. By your grace, and with the power of the Holy Spirit, help us to follow and trust the better way of Jesus. Amen.

*Reading from the Psalms:* Read aloud Psalm 25:6-7
*Silence*
*Scripture Reading:* Read aloud Hebrews 1:1-3a.
*Silence*
*Prayer for Guidance:*

Guide us, O God, that we may be so bold to wonder out loud about your glory and love. You, who are greater than we can imagine, are yet closer than we can comprehend. Help us to seek and follow you as made known through the love of Jesus. Amen.

## Video and Discussion (15 minutes)

Introduce the Session 2 video by reviewing the format. The video is six to eight minutes long and is made up of three parts:
- Voices answering a question
- Story by Rueben Job
- Hosted presentation

After watching the video, lead the group in a discussion:
- What or who stood out to you as you heard the voices?
- As you listened to the story about Anna, what thoughts did you have about questions of faith?
- How did you experience the question "Who is God?"

## Book Discussion (15 minutes)

Choose one of the following:

### Group Reflection

Have participants turn to pages 27 and 29 of *Three Simple Questions,* where the following quotations can be found. Using the book or the paragraphs below, read the quotations aloud twice while group members listen, then divide into groups of three to discuss the reflection question that follows. Allow five or ten minutes for these triad discussions, and then invite the whole group to re-gather for the remainder of the time allotted and a shared discussion of the question.

Our Christian creeds all declare our belief in one God while pointing to numerous sources of self-revelation by this God. We Christians worship a God who is revealed in many ways. . . .

While we proclaim faithfully and boldly our own experience of and trust in God, we do so with humility and gentleness as we learn to live in community of earnest God seekers who may have experienced and come to know God in ways different than our own.

• How does your image of God guide you to live in community with others who understand God differently?

### Silent Reflection and Group Discussion

Have participants turn to "Who Is God?" in *Three Simple Questions* and review the material there during one or two minutes of silence, looking for things that caught their attention on first reading. What words, images, phrases, or paragraphs stopped, puzzled, inspired, or troubled them?

After the review time, invite group members each to share one question, insight, or reflection from the reading. After all who wish to share have done so, then open the discussion by asking, "What did we hear?"

# Spiritual Practice (15 minutes)

*Before moving into the spiritual practice, invite participants to stand and stretch for a moment as a way of transition and refreshment.*

**Leader:** (*read aloud or summarize*)

We now come to the part of our session about particular spiritual practices that can help us explore more deeply our "Three Simple Questions." Today's practice is attentiveness. The question "Who is God?" invites us to grow in attentiveness to God's presence in our lives and in the world. The following practice is designed to guide us into more focused attentiveness to God.

*Slowly read the following instructions to participants, giving time for each to be followed. As leader, you will need to pay attention to the time limit.*

### A Spiritual Practice of Attentiveness

- Get into a comfortable position in which you can stay for at least ten minutes. You may stand, sit, or lie down, as you prefer.
- Settle into the quiet and find a comfortable rhythm of breathing.
- Now, look at the palms of your hands, look at the inside of each finger, the creases, scars, calluses. Do not hurry through this time. Really pay attention to the inside of your hands. If you would like, touch the surface and outline of each one. Recall what your hands have done for you and for others; whom they have held and consoled; what they have carried and repaired. Simply pay attention to your hands. Do this for at least four minutes
- Now turn your hands over and do the same for the backs of your hands and fingers. Take your time. Recall how you have been an instrument of God's grace through your hands: holding, repairing, carrying, showing, preparing, writing, and creating. Take your time and just notice, again for at least four minutes. Do not hurry this.
- Again, turn your hands over to see your palms and, using one finger, write your name on the palm of one hand. Remember that your name is written on the palms of God's hands (Isaiah 49:16). Imagine this. Imagine the hands of God in whom you believe and seeing your name written there.
- Now, in silence, offer God a prayer of gratitude for the wonderful image in which you are created.

After this time of practice, lead the group in a brief conversation about how they experienced this practice. What came to mind? Were any prayers formed during the quiet time? Close by saying, "Amen."

## *Prayer Practice (15 minutes)

The following handout may be photocopied for group use:

## Prayer of Imagination

As we boldly and honestly ask, "Who is God?," Rueben Job reminds us, "God is greater than anything we can comprehend or imagine," and yet as human beings we can use our God-given imaginations to help free us from old, restrictive, and sometimes hurtful images of God. So the prayer for this week is a prayer of imagination.

Read once through the following guide, and then enter into silence and follow the steps listed.

- Get into a comfortable position in which you can relax. Breathe in and out deeply and slowly. Become quiet and still.
- Read the following Scripture text in silence. (Feel free to use other Scriptures as well.)

At that place [Elijah] came to a cave, and spent the night there. Then the word of the LORD came to him saying, "What are you doing here Elijah?" He answered, "I have been very zealous for the LORD, the God of hosts; for the Israelites have forsaken your covenant, thrown down your altars, and killed your prophets with the sword. I alone am left, and they are seeking my life, to take it away." He said, "Go out and stand on the mountain before the LORD, for the LORD is about to pass by." Now there was a great wind, so strong that it was splitting mountains and breaking rocks in pieces before the LORD, but the LORD was not in the wind; and after the wind an earthquake, but the LORD was not in the earthquake; and after the earthquake a fire, but the LORD was not in the fire; and after the fire a sound of sheer silence. When Elijah heard it, he wrapped his face in his mantle and went out and stood at the entrance of the cave. (1 Kings 19:9-13)

- Wait for a moment. Read the text again.
- Close your eyes and allow yourself to enter into the scene described in the reading. Imagine with all of your senses what it would be like to be beside Elijah on the mountain ledge waiting for God to pass by. Stay with this image for at least ten minutes and really look, hear, smell, taste, and feel the scene. After ten minutes (your leader will prompt you), open your eyes. If you wish, make notes of what you experienced in the prayer.
- After your prayer and journaling or silent reflection time, close by saying "Amen."

If praying in a group, engage in conversation with others about how you experienced this prayer practice.

## *Creative Practice (20-30 minutes)

Each participant will need a clean index card and a pen or pencil. Ask the group members to draw two lines in the shape of a cross at the center of the index card, dividing the card into four sections.

Next, instruct the group members to write a word or short phrase in each square on the card in response to the following instructions. Deliver the instructions one at a time, pausing for people to think and write before you move on to the next. Do not hurry this process.

In the upper-right box, write the name of something in nature that reminds you of God.

- In the lower-right box, name a sound that reminds you of God.
- In the upper-left box, name a color that reminds you of God.
- In the lower-left box, name a place that helps you feel close to God.
- In the center of the card, write Amen.

After everyone is finished, invite group members to discuss as a group what came to mind during this practice.

## Closing: Reflection and Prayer (5-10 minutes)

Invite participants into a closing time for the session by asking them to choose one word that represents something about who God is for them. Give them a moment of silence in which to identify their word, and begin by sharing your word first. Again, remind them that no word is wrong or right, too big or too little, too different or too similar. It simply needs to be their own word. Go around the group until all have spoken or passed.

*Closing Prayers:* Ask if there are any prayers to be shared in the group, and receive these.
*Lord's Prayer*: Pray together.
*Blessing: May the love of God, the peace of Christ, and the companionship of the Holy Spirit be with us all. Go in peace.*

As participants prepare to depart, remind them to read "Who Am I?" from *Three Simple Questions* in preparation for the next session.

# Session 3
# Who Am I?

## Before the Group Meets

Prayerfully read "Who Am I?" from *Three Simple Questions*, as well as the material in this leader guide for Session 3. Preview the video segment for Session 3.

**For Session 3 the participant will need:**
- A copy of *Three Simple Questions*
- Pen or pencil
- Journal, notebook, or writing paper

**For Session 3 the leader will need:**
- A plan for how the room should be set up for the session
- A few extra copies of *Three Simple Questions*
- Candle for prayer times, and a lighter or matches
- DVD player and monitor
- At least one Bible (recommend Common English Bible)
- Pencils and pens
- Extra paper for notes

- (Optional) If your group will be doing the Prayer Practice, prepare handout copies of "Breath Prayer."
- (Optional) If your group will be doing the Creative Practice, bring a large clear plastic cup and a blank sheet of paper for each person.
- (Optional) Light refreshments if the group leader desires to provide any

*Note that activities not included in the basic 60-minute format are marked below with an asterisk (\*). However, leaders are free to use any of the activities best suited to their group's time constraints and learning styles.*

## Opening Welcome and Prayer (5 minutes)

**Leader:** (*read aloud or summarize*)

Session 3 of this study encourages us to examine the deeply significant yet simple question, "Who Am I?" In the eyes and heart of the One in whose image I am created and who has given me particular and unique identities, who am I? We will explore through reading and conversation how, in a rushed and too often ruthless culture, we can learn to remember who we are as children of the God of love, revealed to us in Jesus Christ.

Now let us enter into prayer together as we light our candle, a symbol of Christ's steadfast presence and grace.

### Liturgy

*Opening Prayer:*

We welcome you, O God, into this time we spend together, that as our questions are spoken and answers come to light and life, we may listen for you through and with each other. By your grace, and with the power of the Holy Spirit, help us follow and trust the better way of Jesus. Amen.

*Reading from the Psalms:* Read aloud Psalm 139:13-16.

*Silence*

*Scripture Reading:* Read aloud John 3:1-2.
*Silence*
*Prayer for Guidance:*
> God of light, cast your grace on the path before us that we may find our way to you and to the ways of becoming who we are created to be. When we stray or stumble, when we deny or distract, help us to listen for your call to find our way home to you, where we are reminded who and whose we are. Amen.

## Video and Discussion (15 minutes)

Introduce the Session 3 video by reviewing the format. The video is six to eight minutes long and is made up of three parts:
- Voices answering a question
- Story by Rueben Job
- Hosted presentation

After watching the video, lead the group in a discussion:
- What or who stands out to you as you heard the voices?
- After listening to the story, what helps you to remember who you really are as a follower of Christ?
- Who was the first person to tell you that you are a beloved child of God?

## Book Discussion (15 minutes)
Choose one of the following:

### Group Reflection

Ask participants to turn to page 46 of *Three Simple Questions,* where the following quotation can be found. Read the quotation aloud twice, with a brief time of silence in between the readings. After the second reading, invite the whole group to respond to the discussion question below:

> When we forget who we are and begin to see others as anything less than beloved children of God, we are giving up our identity and our inheritance as children of God.

- What contributes to our individual and collective forgetfulness that we are children of God? Discuss current and specific examples.

**Silent Reflection and Group Discussion**

Have the participants turn to "Who Am I?" in *Three Simple Questions* and review the material there during one or two minutes of silence, looking for things that caught their attention on first reading. Are there words, images, phrases, or paragraphs that stopped, puzzled, inspired, or troubled them?

After the review time, invite group members each to share one question, insight, or reflection from the reading. Before sharing begins, suggest that the group use this time to practice listening rather than responding. You may want to start by offering your own insight or question. After all who wish to share have done so, then open the discussion by asking, "What did we hear?"

# Spiritual Practice (15 minutes)

*Before moving into the spiritual practice, invite participants to stand and stretch for a moment as a way of transition and refreshment.*

**Leader:** (*read aloud or summarize*)

We now come to the part of our session about particular spiritual practices that can help us explore more deeply our "Three Simple Questions." Today's practice is journaling. The practice of journaling, whether through poetry, prose, sketching, or prayer, can offer a way, honestly and prayerfully, to "author" elements of our personal story about life with God and neighbor. For this practice, we will each need a journal, notebook, or writing paper, as well as a pen or pencil.

*Slowly read the following instructions to participants, giving time for each to be followed. As leader, you will need to pay attention to the time limit.*

## A Spiritual Practice of Journaling

- Take your paper or journal to a comfortable place in the room where you can write or draw.
- Settle into the quiet and find a comfortable rhythm of breathing.
- You will be asked to complete a sentence during this journaling practice, and you will have ten minutes to do so by writing or drawing. Journaling can take many forms.
- Complete the following sentence using words or pictures. You will not be asked to share what you have done.

As a child of God, when I reflect on the phrase "our full inheritance from God,"

I think about _____.

- After the time is complete, as leader, close this practice by offering "Amen."

# *Prayer Practice (15 minutes)

The following handout may be photocopied for group use:

# Breath Prayer

There are many prayer forms that can help us pray the question "Who am I?" But a breath prayer, by its very name and nature, is an excellent practice to help us live into the question. A breath prayer is personal, repeated, and rhythmic, as is our own rhythm of breathing in and out. And a breath prayer teaches us to combine in prayer "who God is" with "who we are" in a particular way and practice.

Read once through the following guide, and then enter into silence and follow the steps listed.

- Get into a comfortable position. Breathe in and out deeply and slowly. Do all that you can to become still and quiet.
- Select a name for God that you would like to use today in your prayer. You could choose God, Lord, Holy Spirit, Loving Jesus, Tender Shepherd, Abba, Mother/Father God, Jesus Christ, or any name for God that you wish. Take a minute to say it quietly to yourself over and over again.
- Now, imagine Jesus asking you: "What is your deepest longing right now, in this moment?" Do not edit your answer, but listen for it. Is your longing for rest, peace, courage, healing? Take a minute or two to name your longing.
- Finally, create a short prayer, a breath prayer, by combining your name for God and your deepest longing in some ordered phrase that you can easily repeat. Some examples are:

> O Christ, give me courage.
> Help me find rest, O Shepherd.
> Holy Spirit, heal my heart.

- Remember, this is *your* breath prayer. When you are ready, close your eyes and repeat the prayer over and over, breathing and praying in and out.
- After an extended time (at least ten minutes) end with "Amen."

If praying in a group, engage in conversation with others about how you experienced this prayer practice.

## *Creative Practice (20-30 minutes)

Each participant will need a clear plastic cup, a clean sheet of paper, and a pen or pencil. First, ask group members to hold their empty cup in both hands in front of them and to listen as you read from pages 41-42 of "Who Am I?" in *Three Simple Questions*:

> In John 14:23, Jesus reminds us that we are invited to become a holy chalice in which God chooses to dwell: "Whoever loves me will keep my word. My Father will love them, and we will come to them and make our home with them." Even before we are fully aware of this truth, we are already claimed as children of God. We were made in God's image, and God chooses to dwell within us.

Now, ask group members to imagine their cup as a chalice representing their own life. Invite them to envision the divine presence, energy, wisdom, and direction that God wants each of them to have and hold in the chalice of their life.

After a minute of silence, instruct group members to set the cups aside, then write on their paper a list of blessings, qualities, and gifts that God has given them. Invite them to use this time to affirm ways in which God chooses to dwell in each of them, individually and uniquely, through people, talents, gifts, call, or experiences that bring joy and love. Provide at least fifteen minutes for this list. Encourage group members to write down as many things as come to mind in the time given.

After fifteen minutes, instruct them to fold their paper and place it into their chalice, then offer "Amen."

End this practice by inviting any who wish to do so to share what they experienced during this practice.

## Closing: Reflection and Prayer (5-10 minutes)

Invite participants into a closing time for the session by asking them to express in one word a blessing or spiritual gift they have been given by God. Begin by sharing your own word, and then go around the group until all have spoken.

*Closing Prayers:* Ask if there are any prayers to be shared in the group, and receive these.

*Lord's Prayer:* Pray together.

*Blessing:* May the love of God, the call of Jesus, and the power of the Holy Spirit guide us all. Go in peace.

As participants prepare to depart, remind them to read "Who Are We Together?" from *Three Simple Questions* in preparation for the next session.

# Session 4
# Who Are We Together?

## Before the Group Meets

Prayerfully read "Who Are We Together?" in *Three Simple Questions,* as well as the material in this leader guide for Session 4. Preview the video segment for Session 4.

**For Session 4 the participant will need:**
- A copy of *Three Simple Questions*
- Pen or pencil
- Journal, notebook, or writing paper

**For Session 4 the leader will need:**
- A plan for how the room should be set up for the session
- A few extra copies of *Three Simple Questions*
- Candle for prayer times, and a lighter or matches
- DVD player and monitor
- At least one Bible (recommend Common English Bible)
- Pencils and pens
- Extra paper for notes

- (Optional) If your group will be doing the Prayer Practice, prepare handout copies of "Prayer of Examen."
- (Optional) If your group will be doing the Creative Practice, bring a sheet of drawing paper for each participant and enough coloring pencils or markers for the group to share (at least two per person).
- (Optional) Light refreshments if the group leader desires to provide any

*Note that activities not included in the basic 60-minute format are marked below with an asterisk (\*). However, leaders are free to use any of the activities best suited to their group's time constraints and learning styles.*

## Opening Welcome and Prayer (5 minutes)

**Leader:** (*read aloud or summarize*)

Session 4 guides us toward a conversation about the difficulty and reward of living in community, by considering the question "Who Are We Together?" In *Three Simple Questions,* Rueben Job writes for us about multiple dimensions of living together in the world God loves. There is the dimension of being part of the human family—diverse, extended, global, but all one in the eyes of our Creator. There is the dimension of being part of a faith family—beloved and called and equally precious to God, but wonderfully unique in our experiences and understanding of the divine. And there is the dimension for Christians of seeking to be Christ-followers—challenging, trying, trusting, and realizing we cannot do it on our own. These are some of the issues we will explore in this session.

So, let us continue together by entering into a time of silence as we light the candle as a symbol of Christ in our midst, and prepare to be in prayer.

**Liturgy**

*Opening Prayer:*
> We welcome you, O God, into this time we spend together, that as our questions are spoken and answers come to light and life, we may listen for you through and with each other. By your grace, and with the power of the Holy Spirit, help us to follow and trust the better way of Jesus. Amen.

*Reading from Psalms:* Read aloud Psalm 145:8-9.
*Silence*
*Scripture Reading:* Read aloud Ephesians 4:1b-4, followed by a minute of silence.
*Silence*
*Prayer for Guidance:*
> Loving God, we thank you that the light of your grace is cast wider and deeper and higher than any light we can make or cast on our own. We thank you that the light of your grace finds each of us wherever we are and shines on a path to you and toward each other. We thank you that over and over again you show us the better way of Jesus—our light and path and guide. Amen.

# Video and Discussion (15 minutes)

Introduce the Session 4 video by reviewing the format. The video is six to eight minutes long and is made up of three parts:
- Voices answering a question
- Story by Rueben Job
- Hosted presentation

After watching the video, lead the group in a discussion:
- What or who stood out to you as you heard the voices?
- What role does loving community play in your life?
- How do you respond to the word *family*?

# Book Discussion (15 minutes)
Choose one of the following:

## Group Reflection

Have participants turn to page 57 of *Three Simple Questions*, where the following quotation can be found. Using the book or the paragraph below, read the quotation aloud twice while group members listen. After the second reading, invite the whole group to reflect together on the questions that follow.

> There seems to have been an eclipse of what we Christians hold in common with all people as we use markers to distinguish ourselves or separate ourselves from the larger human family. Each division only makes it more difficult to remember who we are as God's beloved children.

- What are some of the markers used today to distinguish Christians from the "larger human family"? Name both positive and negative markers of which you are aware.
- Where do we see hopeful, purposeful signs of reconciliation and restoration of the larger human family?
- How is the Christian community participating in this reconciliation and restoration? Be specific.

## Silent Reflection and Group Discussion

Have participants turn to "Who Are We Together?" in *Three Simple Questions* and review the material there during one or two minutes of silence, looking for things that caught their attention on first reading. What words, images, phrases, or paragraphs stopped, puzzled, inspired, or troubled them?

After the review time, invite group members each to share one question, insight, or reflection from the reading. Before sharing begins, suggest that the group use this time to practice listening rather than responding. You may want to start by offering your own insight or question. After all who wish to share have done so, then open the discussion by asking, "What did we hear?"

# Spiritual Practice (15 minutes)

*Before moving into the spiritual practice, invite participants to stand and stretch for a moment as a way of transition and refreshment.*

**Leader:** (read aloud or summarize)

We come again to the time in our session to share in a spiritual practice that can help us see facets of our "three simple questions" that we might otherwise miss. Today's practice is *Lectio Divina,* sacred reading of Scripture, and for our purpose we will read only one part of a verse, a part that may seem small but that radiates more than we dare imagine if we seek to understand, meditate, and risk its implications for our life together.

On page 62 of *Three Simple Questions,* Rueben Job cites Matthew 4:19a, and then asks us faithfully and honestly to consider how we can get beyond division and being "stuck in our own ways." He suggests that one way to do so is by "deepening our practice of prayer and meditation upon Scripture."

The practice of Lectio Divina combines both prayer and meditation, and Matthew 4:19a is a good place to start as we continue to ask, "Who Are We Together?"

*Use the following guide to lead your group members through this practice for about eight minutes. It will be helpful to describe all the steps first before you lead the practice.*

## A Spiritual Practice of Lectio Divina[4]

- Invite group members to settle comfortably in their seats, feet on the floor, and to find a relaxed rhythm of breathing. Some may wish to close their eyes.
- Tell the group that you will read a Scripture to them two times. The first time, they are to listen for the meaning of the entire passage; the second time, they are to listen for a word or phrase that attracts them. In the silence that follows your reading, invite them to repeat their word silently. After one minute, but not before, invite them to speak their word or phrase out loud

but to not say anything else yet. Even if others say the same word or phrase, encourage them to say it too.

- Read the text a third time, and instruct group members to listen for a way in which the Scripture touches their lives right now. Give them two minutes to consider this question: How does this passage from Scripture touch your life? They may share a sentence or two in response this time. If they need help doing so, encourage them to describe what they feel, see, hear, or imagine in response to the Scripture.
- After all who wish to have shared, read the text a fourth time. Ask group members to listen for an invitation that can be lived out in the next day or two. What is this Scripture inviting them to do in the very near future? After two or three minutes, invite sharing of individual invitations that have been received.
- Finally, ask people to pray silently for the group member on their right, that the invitation heard may be received.

In the remaining time, engage participants in a conversation about how they experienced this spiritual practice.

## *Prayer Practice (15 minutes)

The following handout copy may be photocopied for group use:

# Prayer of Examen

On page 58 of *Three Simple Questions,* Rueben Job writes:

> Honesty requires us to invite God's Spirit to examine us and see where, how, and when we contribute to our brokenness as the body of Christ. What is it in us that makes it so difficult to see others as children of God who are loved by God and accepted by God as we believe we are loved and accepted by God?

A prayer practice that can help us become more honest before God with the help of God's Spirit is the prayer of Examen. The Examen is a daily practice during which we examine our thoughts, feelings, and actions of the day in light of God's presence and our response. Some call this a daily spiritual inventory and find it most useful at bedtime, but it may be used at any time of day to review the past twenty-four hours of one's life, placing all of it before God's gentle grace.

- Read once through the following guide, and then enter into silence and follow the steps listed.
- Get into a comfortable position. If you would like, place your hand over your heart. Recall the past twenty-four hours of your life, not through analysis but in the form of a gentle review. Just listen for and notice what comes up for you.
- Now ask yourself: Where in the day were you most grateful? When was your faith strong and loving? How was God present to you in those times? Be grateful.
- Next ask yourself: Where in the day were you least grateful? When were you alienated from God or neighbor? How could God have been more present to you? Ask for God's forgiveness and mercy, and for God's help in the day to come.
- Finally, turn the day over to God, every part of it, and accept God's love and compassion for you. Breathe in the love of God and remember that you are God's beloved. Then rest.

If you are with a group, spend some time in conversation about how you experienced this prayer practice.

# *Creative Practice (20-30 minutes)

Each participant will need a clean sheet of drawing paper and access to a set of colored markers or pencils that have been placed in the center or front of the group for easy access. Explain that group members will work in silence until you invite them, at the end, into a time of sharing. Then invite participants, a few at a time, to select one or two pencils or markers.

Now, ask them to draw a very basic map of the city in which they live. This may be done by simply marking on the paper five or six locations of daily importance for them—nothing elaborate, just a sketch will do. Give them about five minutes to do this.

Next, read this quotation, taken from page 63 of *Three Simple Questions*: "But how do we remain in Christ's presence? . . . Are we seeking his presence in the sacred places of life where he was found during his days on earth?"

As the participants reflect on these words, invite them to turn to the person beside them and share, for about ten minutes, how Christ is present in some of the daily places on their "map." Encourage them to talk with each other about what difference it makes or could make to remember that Christ is in these "sacred places of life."

# Closing: Reflection and Prayer (5-10 minutes)

Invite participants into a closing time for the session by asking each person to choose one word about loving a neighbor as oneself. As before, begin by sharing your word, then go around the group until all have spoken.

*Closing Prayers*: Ask if there are any prayers to be shared in the group, and receive these.
*Lord's Prayer:* Pray together.
*Blessing:* May companionship with Christ lead us to be companions with one another. May a fresh burst of the Holy Spirit awaken us to life and faithfulness anew. Go in peace.

As participants prepare to depart, instruct them to read the Epilogue of *Three Simple Questions* for the next session.

# Session 5
# Praying the Questions

## Before the Group Meets

Prayerfully read the Epilogue in *Three Simple Questions,* as well as the material in this leader guide for Session 5. Preview the video segment for Session 5.

**For Session 5 the participant will need:**
- A copy of *Three Simple Questions*
- Pen or pencil
- Journal, notebook, or writing paper

**For Session 5 the leader will need:**
- A plan for how the room should be set up for the session
- A few extra copies of *Three Simple Questions*
- Candle for prayer times, and a lighter or matches
- DVD player and monitor
- At least one Bible (recommend Common English Bible)
- Pencils and pens
- Extra paper for notes
- (Optional) If your group will be doing the Prayer Practice, prepare handout copies of "Moving Prayer."

- (Optional) Light refreshments if the group leader desires to provide them

*Note that activities not included in the basic 60-minute format are marked below with an asterisk (\*). However, leaders are free to use any of the activities best suited to their group's time constraints and learning styles.*

## Opening Welcome and Prayer (5 minutes)

**Leader:** (*read aloud or summarize*)

Session 5 of our study has two intended purposes: first, to carefully review and examine the Epilogue of *Three Simple Questions,* which serves almost as a benediction for this study; and second, to further shape us into people of prayer who are not afraid to ask the three simple questions, recognizing the questions as holy invitations to draw closer to God, our Creator, for whom no questions are too great or too small. In this session we will be guided by the ideas in the Epilogue and by various experiences and forms of prayer.

As before, let us now prepare to be in prayer together as we light our Christ candle, a symbol of God's ever-present love, hope, and purpose made known through Jesus Christ.

### Liturgy

*Opening Prayer:*
We welcome you, O God, into this time we spend together, that as our questions are spoken and answers come to light and life, we may listen for you through and with each other. By your grace, and with the power of the Holy Spirit, help us to follow and trust the better way of Jesus. Amen.
*Reading from Psalms:* Read aloud Psalm 64:1-4.
*Silence*
*Scripture Reading:* Read aloud Luke 11:1-4.
*Silence*

*Prayer for Guidance:*
God of day and night, of parable and commandment, we thank you for teaching us to pray in many ways, times, and places. You are the sound of sheer silence and of falling water. You are the burning bush and the shade beneath an eagle's wing. You are never far and never turned away from us. Hear our prayers, O God. Help us to pray. Amen.

## Video and Discussion (15 minutes)

Introduce the Session 5 video by reviewing the format. The video is six to eight minutes long and is made up of three parts:
- Voices answering a question
- Story by Rueben Job
- Hosted presentation

After watching the video, lead the group in a discussion:
- What or who stood out to you as you heard the voices?
- What role does prayer play in your life?
- What helps you "do your part" for God's world as a member of the living body of Christ?

## Book Discussion (15 minutes)
Choose one of the following:

### Group Reflection

Ask participants to turn to page 46 of *Three Simple Questions,* where the following quotation can be found. Using the book or the paragraph below, read the quotation aloud twice while group members listen, then divide into groups of three to discuss the reflection question that follows. Allow five or ten minutes for these triad discussions, and then invite the whole group to re-gather for the remainder of the time allotted and a shared discussion of the question.

Prayer helps us to know who we are and where we find the nurture, comfort, guidance, courage, and strength to live as children of God—bringing love, justice, peace, and reward. The reward is knowing who we are and claiming our inheritance as children of God—an inheritance that no one can take from us and that we cannot take from another.

- Recall a time when prayer helped you remember and know who you are. What role did prayer play at the time?

**Silent Reflection and Group Discussion**

Have participants turn to the Epilogue of *Three Simple Questions* and review the material there during one or two minutes of silence, looking for things that caught their attention on first reading. What words, images, phrases, or paragraphs stopped, puzzled, inspired, or troubled them?

After the review time, invite each group member to share one question, insight, or reflection from the reading. Before sharing begins, suggest that the group use this time to practice listening rather than responding. You may want to start by offering your own insight or question. After all who wish to share have done so, then open the discussion by asking, "What did we hear?"

# Spiritual Practice (15 minutes)

Before moving into the spiritual practice, invite participants to stand and stretch for a moment as a way of transition and refreshment.

**Leader:** (*read aloud or summarize*)

As we prepare to experience the spiritual practice for this session, once again we are asked to keep the "three simple questions" before us. The practice for today is Unceasing Prayer (see 1 Thessalonians 5:17).

Continual prayer seems impossible to many of us, and yet our three simple questions can serve as windows flung wide open into prayer with God. We live with these questions all the time at some level of our soul, and when we allow the questions to live near the surface and seek to bring them into the light, how can they not involve prayer? As long as we are faithful in remembering that we are not God, and yet are created in the image of God, then we become free to express our questions, wonders, doubts, and longings in prayer—not as failed quests for answers but as acknowledgment that we are created to ask, seek, receive, and change by the grace of God. This acknowledgment is at the heart of Unceasing Prayer.

*Slowly read the following instructions to participants, giving time for each to be followed. As leader, you will need to pay attention to the time limit.*

### Unceasing Prayer

- Get as comfortable as you can in your chair, or if you wish to walk or stand during this practice, that is fine. Once you have a comfortable posture, quiet your breathing to a pace and rhythm that you find relaxing.
- Listen to each of the following three questions and let them become a prayer for you, with or without answer. Practice praying the question over and over again, and be gentle with yourself in the process. Resist insisting on a single answer; rather, allow multiple and differing responses to come to you
- Let us pray: O God, who are you?
  (Give at least 3 minutes for this question)
- Let us pray: O God, who am I to you and to myself and to others?
  (Give at least 3 minutes for this question)
- Let us pray: O God, who are we together, you and I and my neighbors?
  (Give at least 3 minutes for this question)

As there is time, ask the group to discuss briefly their experience of praying the questions in this way.

## *Prayer Practice (15 minutes)
The following handout may be photocopied for group use:

## Moving Prayer

Prayer is not only about silence and sitting; prayer is a way of living. God's world is large and expansive and open, and prayer can be and is part of any movement that we make into and through that world. Prayer is our first language, our primary language with the One who longs to be in communion and communication with us wherever we are. So this practice, recognizing our daily movements as opportunities to be in prayer, will help us learn to pray continually.

- For this experience of prayer, you will be invited to move around the room, around the building, or outside the building for the next ten minutes or so. Where you go will, of course, depend on your setting, but go where you can.
- When you move, remember that you are a chalice for the living, praying Spirit of God, and that as you move you carry with you the prayers and questions of your life and of those who have entrusted their prayers to you. These prayers are written on your heart and go with you.
- As you are ready, and keeping track of the time, walk, stretch, run, move where you can, and actively remember that as you do, these prayers will go with you.
- You may want to recall a different person each time you walk down a hall, lifting that person's life and needs during each lap of the hallway. You can do the same on a city block or on trips across a room. You can lift each prayer to God in a stretch or in every few steps.
- The purpose of this prayer practice is to help you get in touch with different postures and movements of prayer, especially those that are already part of your daily life.

Remember that you can continue Moving Prayers in your individual setting whether walking, jogging, swimming, shopping, washing dishes, knitting, cooking, driving, or any other daily movements.

After ten minutes, return to the group, and share in conversation about this and other forms of prayer in which movement is key.

# *Creative Practice (20-30 minutes)

Each participant will need their copy of *Three Simple Questions* and their notebook or journal. Ask them to read silently the three prayers in *Three Simple Questions* on pages 32, 49, and 69. Once all have completed this reading, ask them to look up toward you so that you know when they have finished.

Now, ask if anyone recalls the last line of each prayer. If not, remind them that each prayer ends with "in the name and Spirit of Jesus Christ" or "in the name and Spirit of Christ."

For the next fifteen minutes, invite group members to write about what this means to them: to pray in the name and Spirit of Jesus Christ. As Christians, what difference does it make to their understanding of prayer? What does the name of Jesus Christ bring to our prayers? What does the Spirit of Christ bring to our prayers?

After the silent writing time, bring the whole group back together for discussion.

# Closing: Reflection and Prayer (5-10 minutes)

Invite participants into a closing time by asking them to choose one color that describes their prayer life at this time. Give them a few moments of silence to think about it. Begin by sharing your color, then go around the room asking all who wish to share the color they chose to do so.

*Closing Prayers:* Ask if there are any prayers to be shared in the group and receive these.
*Lord's Prayer:* Pray together.
*Blessing:* May you hope in the Lord who made and makes heaven and earth, who is your refuge and strength in times of trouble and joy. May you lift your prayers to the Lord, shepherd, guardian, and guide. Go in peace.

As participants prepare to depart, ask them to re-read the Preface to *Three Simple Questions* for the last session.

# Session 6
# Living the Questions

## Before the Group Meets

Prayerfully re-read the Preface to *Three Simple Questions,* as well as the material in this leader guide for Session 6. Preview the video segment for Session 6.

**For Session 6 the participant will need:**
- A copy of *Three Simple Questions*
- Pen or pencil
- Journal, notebook, or writing paper

**For Session 6 the leader will need:**
- A plan for how the room should be set up for the session
- few extra copies of *Three Simple Questions*
- Candle for prayer times, and a lighter or matches
- DVD player and monitor
- At least one Bible (recommend Common English Bible)
- Pencils and pens
- Extra paper for notes

- (Optional) Light refreshments if the group leader desires to provide any

*Note that activities not included in the basic 60-minute format are marked below with an asterisk (\*). However, leaders are free to use any of the activities best suited to their group's time constraints and learning styles.*

# Opening Welcome and Prayer (5 minutes)

**Leader:** (*read aloud or summarize*)

Our final group session brings to a close our small-group experience in which we have prayed, practiced, and reflected together on three simple yet profound questions of faith:
- Who is God?
- Who am I?
- Who are we together?

Today we will recall and draw upon our experiences of the past five sessions and on how, through conversation, practice, and prayer, these three simple questions can become instruments of love, hope, and purpose in the Christian spiritual life. Although we returned to where we began, the Preface of *Three Simple Questions,* we find that we have already been changed by our commitment to live the questions together.

So one last time we light our candle, a symbol of God's love and light, a sign of God's love for us revealed in Jesus Christ who is the light of the world.

## Liturgy

*Opening Prayer:*

We welcome you, O God, into this time we spend together, that as our questions are spoken and answers come to light and life, we may listen for you through and with each other. By your grace, and with the power of the Holy Spirit, help us follow and trust the better way of Jesus. Amen.

*Reading from the Psalms:* Read aloud Psalm 40:1-5.
*Silence*
*Scripture Reading:* Read aloud Ephesians 5:1-2a.
*Silence*
*Prayer for Guidance:*
> Gentle Shepherd, help us to know your voice no matter the noise, clamor, and distractions we confront. Help us to trust that even when we wander off or away, you still search for us, miss us, and make a place for us to help your kingdom come on earth as it is in heaven. Amen.

## Video and Discussion (15 minutes)

Introduce the Session 6 video by reviewing the format. The video is six to eight minutes long and is made up of three parts:
- Voices answering a question
- Story by Rueben Job
- Hosted presentation

After watching the video, lead the group in a discussion:
- What or who stood out to you as you heard the voices?
- In what ways do you sense God nudging you at this moment to embody Christ's love in the world?
- What is one way, practice, or relationship that can keep you mindful of the three simple questions and the way they point to God's love?

## Book Discussion (15 minutes)

### Group Reflection – Option A

Ask group members to turn to page 10 of Three Simple Questions, where the following quotation can be found. Using the book or the paragraph below, read the quotation aloud twice while the group listens.

> Because I believe most of us do want to live a life of faithfulness and fidelity, I also believe that we are ready to once again get

serious about our understanding of who God is, who we are, who we are together, and how we should live as creatures of the Creator God who has made all that is.

Ask participants to form groups of three to discuss the quotation. Do they agree? Why or why not? What are signs of readiness and desire for a new understanding and way of life? They will have five to eight minutes in triads, and then bring the whole group together for another five-to-eight-minute discussion.

## Group Reflection – Option B

Ask group members to turn to page 9 of *Three Simple Questions,* where the following quotation can be found. Using the book or the paragraph below, read the quotation aloud twice while the group listens.

> Our identity is found and formed by the God we worship and serve. Our life together as Christians is discovered, held together, and lived out based on our understanding of the God we have come to know and seek to follow.

Begin a group discussion guided by the questions below:
- During the weeks of this study, what have we discovered or rediscovered about the Christian life?
- What holds our "life together" as Christians?

# *Spiritual Practice (30 minutes)

*Before moving into the spiritual practice, invite participants to stand and stretch for a moment as a way of transition and refreshment.*

**Leader:** (*read aloud or summarize*)

As in previous weeks, this section is designed to help us become familiar with a variety of spiritual practices that can lead us into more faithful living. For each "simple question" in his book, Rueben Job provides a "simple practice." These practices invite us to experience at a fresh level something about the question we are exploring.

For this activity, participants will need their copy of *Three Simple Questions*, which we will use as a guide to each practice. Plan to spend ten minutes with each practice and group reflection.

## Three Simple Practices

Who is God?
A Simple Practice
Invite group members turn to page 31 of *Three Simple Questions* and to read through the simple practice found there. After all have finished reading, lead the group through the practice, reading the instructions aloud. Follow with a brief group reflection time about the practice and about how this practice in particular connects to the question: Who is God?

Who am I?
A Simple Practice
Invite group members turn to page 48 of *Three Simple Questions* and to read through the simple practice found there. After all have finished reading, lead the group through the practice. Follow with a brief group reflection time about the practice and about how this practice in particular connects to the question: Who am I?

Who are we together?
A Simple Practice
Invite group members turn to page 68 of *Three Simple Questions* and to read through the simple practice found there. After all have finished reading, lead the group through the practice. Follow with a brief group reflection time about the practice and about how this practice in particular connects to the question: Who are we together?

*For Session 6, the last activity before closing is a conversation about living the three simple questions. Group leaders will need to watch the clock carefully so there will be time left for the closing.*

## Three Simple Questions: A Conversation (20 minutes)

**Leader:** (*read aloud or summarize*)

Our final session does not include a prayer practice, but asks instead that we end with a prayerful conversation about what we have experienced and learned during this study. This is time for open conversation in which we share insights, learnings, or questions prompted by *Three Simple Questions* and by our life together as we explored, risked, and prayed the questions. With that in mind, ask the group to discuss the following questions:
- What has this time together helped you to understand about God?
- What has this time together helped you to understand about yourself, as a child of God?
- What has this time together helped you to understand about being part of the body of Christ in the world that God loves?

## Closing: Reflection and Prayer (5-10 minutes)

Ask participants to recall the three simple questions:
- Who is God?
- Who am I?
- Who are we together?

Invite each person to share one word that these questions now bring to mind.

*Closing Prayers:* Ask if there are any prayers to be shared and receive them.
*Lord's Prayer:* Pray together.
*Blessing:* May you leave, confident that you are God's beloved child; that you are created in the image of the God of love, hope, and holy purpose; and that you are called and encouraged by our Lord Jesus Christ, through the power of the most Holy Spirit, to claim your full inheritance as a follower of Jesus. Go in peace.

# Retreat Options

## One-Day Retreat

| | |
|---|---|
| 9:00 | Gathering |
| | Introduction of *Three Simple Questions* |
| 9:15 | Morning Prayer/Worship |
| 9:30 | Community Time |
| | The Practice of Spiritual Reading, *Lectio Divina* |
| | Summary Presentation: "Who Is God?" |
| 10:15 | Individual Time |
| | Spiritual Reading: "Who Is God?" |
| 11:00 | Community Time |
| | Group Sharing: "Who Is God?" |
| | Summary Presentation: "Who Am I?" |
| 12:00 | Lunch |
| 12:45 | Individual Time |
| | Spiritual Reading: "Who Am I?" |
| 1:30 | Community Time |
| | Group Sharing: "Who Am I?" |
| | Summary Presentation: "Who Are We Together?" |
| 2:30 | Individual Time |
| | Spiritual Reading: "Who Are We Together?" |
| 3:15 | Community Time |
| | Group Sharing: "Who Are We Together?" |
| 4:00 | Closing Prayer/Worship |
| 4:15 | Departure |

# Three-Day Retreat

## Friday

| | |
|---|---|
| 4:00 | Arrival and Settling In |
| 6:00 | Dinner |
| 7:00 | Gathering in Song and Introductions |
| 7:30 | Community Gathers |
| | *Three Simple Questions:* |
| | *Knowing the God of Love, Hope, and Purpose* |
| |     Presentation |
| |     Reflecting/Sharing in Pairs |
| |     Full-Group Dialogue |
| 8:30 | Night Prayer |
| 9:00 | Quiet |

## Saturday

| | |
|---|---|
| 7:30 | Morning Prayer |
| 8:00 | Breakfast |
| 9:00 | Community Gathers: "Who Is God?" |
| |     Presentation |
| |     Reflecting/Sharing in Triads |
| 10:00 | Individual Time: "Who Is God?" |
| |     Reading/Journaling/Reflecting |
| 11:30 | Community Gathers: "Who Is God" |
| |     Full-Group Dialogue |
| 12:00 | Lunch |
| 1:00 | Individual Time: "Who Am I?" |
| |     Reading/Journaling/Reflecting |
| 2:30 | Community Gathers: "Who Am I?" |
| |     Guided Meditation |
| |     Full-Group Dialogue |
| 3:30 | Free Time |
| 5:30 | Evening Prayer |
| 6:00 | Dinner |
| 7:00 | Community Gathers: "Who Are We Together?" |
| |     Presentation |
| |     Personal Reflection |
| |     Reflecting in Small Groups (5-6 participants) |

| | |
|---|---|
| 8:30 | Night Prayer |
| 9:00 | Quiet |

**Sunday**

| | |
|---|---|
| 8:00 | Breakfast |
| 9:00 | Community Gathers |
| | *Three Simple Questions:* |
| | *Knowing the God of Love, Hope, and Purpose* |
| |     Presentation |
| |     Reflecting/Sharing in Triads |
| |     Full-Group Dialogue |
| 10:30 | Individual Time |
| |     Reading/Journaling/Reflecting |
| 11:15 | Community Gathers for Prayer and Communion |
| Noon | Depart |

# Churchwide Study and Intergenerational Activities

To help your congregation explore the ideas in Rueben P. Job's book *Three Simple Questions,* six-week studies are available for three age levels, so that you can create a churchwide program.

**Adults**
- *Three Simple Questions,* by Rueben P. Job
- DVD with Leader Guide

**Youth**
- *Three Simple Questions: A Six-Week Study for Youth*

**Children**
- *Three Simple Questions to Help Children Know God*

As you study *Three Simple Questions* with the adults, youth, and children of your congregation, you may want to plan for group involvement in intergenerational activities. Consider these possibilities:

- Plan a concluding celebration on a Sunday morning that will create a renewed commitment to asking and answering the basic questions of our faith. Recruit adults, youth, and children to offer testimonies about what they learned and practiced during their study.

• Add an intergenerational activity to each session. For example, the combined group might create a group banner for each of the three simple questions. The banners can then be displayed in the sanctuary during a worship service as a reminder of what the groups have learned.

• Make suggestions of songs or hymns that reflect the three simple questions for those who plan the worship services for the weeks following the study. Have someone name the connections to the three simple questions when the songs are sung.

• Prepare a video or skits that illustrate the three simple questions. Involve actors from all age groups.

• Have children, youth, and adults work together to design the worship altar that reflects the meanings of the three simple questions in the lives of Christians.

---

[1] Rueben P. Job, *Three Simple Rules: A Wesleyan Way of Living* (Nashville: Abingdon, 2007), p. 7.

[2] Christine Pohl, "Hospitality, a practice and a way of life," in *Vision,* Spring 2002, 37.

[3] Rueben P. Job, "A Pattern for Personal Prayer Retreat," in *Becoming a Praying Congregation: Churchwide Leadership Tools* (Nashville: Abingdon, 2009), 51.

[4] Adapted from Norvene Vest, "The Group Lectio Process," *Gathered in the Word: Praying the Scripture in Small Groups* (Nashville: Upper Room Books, 1996), 27.